YOU ARE NOT THE MAN I LOVED

A Poetry Collection

JADE DIVAC

Performance Note

Pieces marked with a mic stand icon
were written for performance.

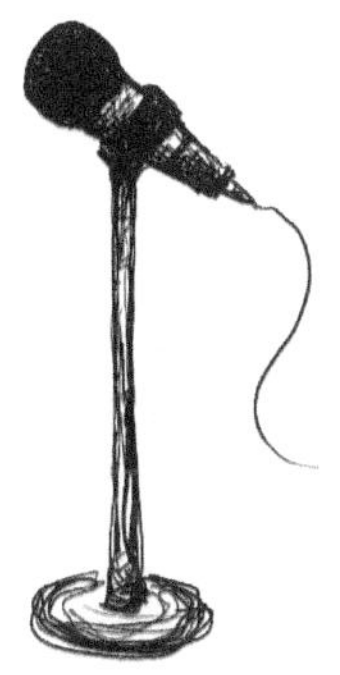

The Five Stages of Grief

Psychologists say
there are five stages of grief,
which you can apply
to heartbreak.
But dig further and you'll see
that the stages
aren't really fixed.

Because we're humans —
not just biology.

The truth is:
Grief is nonlinear.
And healing is too.

If this was love,
hating me would have been a kindness.

The Grief of

NEEDING YOU

Intimate Fantasy

You made me cum
by telling me you loved me
and saying you were all mine.

But as it turns out,
I shouldn't have cum.

Silly me –
I got caught up in the intimacy
of what I didn't realize was a fantasy.

Not My Villain

I don't know that I know
I'm the protagonist in our story.
I feel like the story,
when it leaves my lips,
is a plot synopsis from a movie
I could've never thought up on my own.

I think I'm living someone else's life —
this one isn't mine.
I'm on commercial break
and can't get back to regular programming.
You're not my villain — you're my lover.
Which crew member switched the scripts?
I don't belong in this storyline —
I never auditioned.

Dear god — get me off set!

Home

Even though I wish it wasn't,
my body seems magnetized to yours.
It acts like it belongs to you.
Your body feels like my home.

How do I survive the loss?
Being homeless?
Cut off from the arms that wrapped me up?
The chest I laid my head against in comfort?
The hands that caressed me
and I thought wanted only to deliver me pleasure?

You are the only home I've wanted
for so long,
and I can't help
but want to return to you.

Rest

I thought it would be safe to take you in,
since you had done the same for others.
I didn't blame you for needing a break,
and since able,
I was happy to help.

But you took and took,
and it never stopped.

Now I'm on the other side,
wondering if there was ever love
or if my value to you
was just so you could rest.

Fever Dream

I was the best target you could pick for a long con,
so eager to love and to be known.
Hoping to be fully understood,
I gave you my secrets
and the play-by-play of my inner operations —
years-worth of gold,
mined with therapy.
I felt so seen.
Now I feel so used.
Like chum in the water —
I never stood a chance.
I was living in a fish bowl,
convinced it was the ocean.
Now I'm left to grieve a love I never had,
and you lost your target.
I could have been the love of your life...
if you were only the man
I thought was real.

Flood

Maybe I'll process this pain
with one more poem.
But the sheer amount of poetry
that's escaping me,
like a fire hydrant
flooding a neighborhood street,
gives me little hope
that recovery lies anywhere
around a corner.
Or even somewhere in the distance
of my horizon.

You Are Not the Man I Loved

I Feel Like I'm High

I thought that I've been processing.
That I've visited all five stages.
That I'm working my way through.
      With tears.
      Constant journaling.
      Conversations with supportive friends.
      Trauma-bonding with strangers.
      These poems.
But amidst it all, my world just paused.

It can't be real.
It couldn't be true.
Soon he'll call me, and I'll sigh in the relief
that this was all just a fever dream.
He's real.
He loves me.
Everything is good again.

I feel like I'm high, but I know I'm not.
How long can shock last?
Am I really back to Denial?
After all this pain and processing,
must I go through this all again?

One Last Time

I know I can't afford you
without giving up everything I am.
I'm already so broken.
I don't even know who you are.
But I'm fantasizing about kissing you
one last time.

And one more.

And one more.

And one more.

HATING YOU

You Are Not the Man I Loved

Ash

What does a soft girl do
when she's set on fire,
but she doesn't know how to burn?
Tell me how to combust instead of douse
so I can turn anger to ash
that can blow away absolved.

I'm not healed in my heart,
though my mind says I should be.
I've been wondering why I'm stuck.
Why the pain keeps revisiting randomly
on unscheduled days
or why my heart still stops each time I see
a silver Hyundai go by...

How do I burn it all?
What can feed the sputtering flame inside me,
so desperate to erupt from the pain
of what the one I loved most
decided to put me through?
Where do I aim anger when
I really wish no one harm?

I wish him no harm,
but I wish myself peace.
Peace and freedom.
But I feel like those are hidden in the ash
I don't know how to create.

Go Heal

You told me, "Go heal,"
softly,
as if you weren't the one
who wounded me.

Ambivalence

It's impressive how many emotions
I can feel for you at once.
I'm angry.
I'm hurt.
I am so, so sad.
I miss you.
I want you.
I hate you.
I love you.
I'm upset I ever gave myself to you.

One Night

Some men have loved me better
in one night
than you did in years.

Monsters

You healed me from the monsters of my past,
only to mirror and then outdo them.
Never letting on that you were,
in fact,
the monster of my present.

Masquerade

I was searching so hard for your humanity
that I willed comfort from your lies.

Your masquerade is exquisite.
But you are soulless.

Counterfeit

You absorbed the love
I spent on you.
But it was intended for a man
who has your face,
yet doesn't exist.

Sex Machines

I promoted you to
          my favorite person on the planet.

You demoted me to
          one of your sex machines.

Right to Love

You brought other women into my life
without my consent.
I always called this
a *right to love* relationship,
breakable at any time,
for any reason,
by either party —
not a contract that needs to be timed out.

If we're making work comparisons,
I thought the expectation was set
to not take secondary employment.

You Are Not the Man I Loved

You Love Women

You said you love women:
A feminist's dream.
You agreed men suck
to make us feel safe.
Protected.
Trusting.
Unafraid.

You don't love women —
you love our exploitation.

I Love You

You weaponized *I love you* —
sacred fucking words.
You stripped them of meaning,
while I kept it assigned.

Ask for a favor:
"I love you."
Be a little mean:
"I love you."
Blow past a boundary:
"I love you."

I *loved* you.
You loved that.

You Are Not the Man I Loved

Hurt Women

I slept in a bed you cheated on me in.

And I slept with the woman you cheated on me in it with
while I was lying in a hospital bed,
2 hours and 20 minutes away while you did it.

And as we snuggled down with her two dogs between us
after a late night out at a bar,
where I celebrated the birthday of a woman
thrust into my life in the most painful way possible,
I tried not to envision it in my brain,
even though that's the first image that flashed into my mind
when she gave me a house tour, only hours before.

I wondered about the sheets
and on which side of the bed
you had chosen to forget me for the weekend.
And we did talk about you there,
together in the place you hurt us both.

And she gave me her sorrow,
and I gave her my pain,
and we fell asleep okay.

I didn't have to dream about you that night,
which would have made waking up there with her a terror.
I was spared, and I'm grateful.

You left a shirt there on that visit,
so many months ago.
Your favorite, she had said,
and then proceeded to describe one I'd bought you
not long before for your 31st birthday.

So you did bring me with you.
And you stripped me off,
tossed me on the floor,
and made me watch your lustful sins.

She's buying a firepit for the backyard.
I'll drive over to visit again,
and we'll burn away as much as we can of yours,
as if that toxic smoke might cleanse us.
Her from being used to unknowingly hurt another woman,
and me from loving a man
who seems to only exist to hurt women.

Bait and Switch

I'll never forget how
you fed my dreams of us
with no intention
of ever letting them come to be.

Hard Hat

One mistake was all it took
to empower an excuse
to explore other women's bodies
and collect their love in buckets.

Although I pushed to rectify,
you pulled up the rug
and convinced me all was well.
"We all make mistakes," you said.

If I had known we needed repair work,
I would have shown up in a hard hat,
ready to rebuild what I had damaged
and prove my love.

But what you gained from it
was a justification to weaponize later —
to persuade me that your exploration
was not your fault, but mine.

Nuclear

I was raised for perfection,
but you said I overachieved.
Yet the first time I proved that I was
just as human as you,
you turned my mistake nuclear.
And I'm confused:
Was I never imperfect enough
or never perfect enough
for you?

Dissection Tray

Do you remember when I told you,
heart splayed in a dissection tray,
that my greatest fear
was not dying alone,
but that it was living unloved?

This is why I think
you must have hated me.

I used a scalpel on myself
to share my heart with you.
You picked up the forceps
and took exactly what you wanted
with a gloved hand.

You did it as if pretending
you were taking care
not to disturb the parts of me in repair.

And you let me think
I was in safe hands.
That you and I would stitch me up
to be better than before.

But you made my wounds deeper
when you let me live so long unloved.

Even if you didn't want to love me,
you didn't have to hate me.

Broken

You said you're too broken of a person
to have stood against the intensity of your surroundings.
So broken you caved into decisions
that I'd never consider options.
But I'm broken now too,
more than ever anticipated.
And what's more,
broken by the one I thought would never hurt me.
Yet I know I could never be broken enough
to adopt a path that would destroy not only myself,
but everyone in my path,
including those I placed there.

All I Did Was Love

All I did was love,
but it feels like I'm dead.
If all I did was love,
is loving completely evil?
Did I sin when I sacrificed my heart
to someone I thought
would leave it intact?
He plucked each vein free,
one by one,
slowly,
so I didn't notice.
Until all he had to do was
rip it from my chest and run.

All I did was love.
Why is that what killed me?

Daddy Issues

You and I have daddy issues.
Two hearts cracked in the same place.
I thought safety in a mirrored wound
and a love that wouldn't abandon me the same way.

But I was wrong.

My wound got deeper
the day I opened the door and found
the man you hated
is the man you became.

You Are Not the Man I Loved

Punchline

You are a punchline now.
A joke I make to my detriment
when lightening a discussion
about what I put up with.

Once the love of my life,
now the lowest threshold for standards,
stashed in Hell.

You're a jaw-dropper
when I want a shock-factor.

A comparison to make other women
feel like less of a fool.

You're the matador,
waving red,
as I demonstrate to others
how not to be the bull.

You are the greatest thing
that ever broke me.

The meanest tease
on the playground.

The toughest exam
I ever failed.

I won't forget you —
you'll live on.
And I'll ensure I never entertain
the likes of you again.

New Cells

I write poems about you still
because you changed every part of me.
It's been seven years since I fell for you.
You know how they say your cells regenerate
so that every seven years you're a completely new person?
        I'm a whole new bitch.
If the eyes that lit up when I saw you
are made of new cells now,
if the hands that held your face to mine,
if the body that curved into you
are new,
I can only be relieved.
You changed my brain chemistry.
I'm glad there's nothing physical of you left.

How Dare You

How dare you think
that I was warming the beds of strangers
when I was cleaning their toilets,
packing their dishware,
and color-coding their garments
in my time off
so that you'd want for nothing
while you sat at home,
hooked to a controller and a hookah hose,
engulfed in an endless depression,
and succumbing.

Black Holes

You are the black holes
you fetishize
in the solar systems
of our galaxies.

Are they inspiration to you?
The greatest teachers of
how to swallow up
everything in their horizons
and leave nothing behind,
until all that's left
is the inevitable fate
of succumbing to the gravity
of what they themselves created?

Red Flags

I'm so tired of people telling me I'm stupid
for not knowing all these flags were red.
I had years of trust invested
in someone who had never given me
a reason to doubt him.

We did long, deep, and tearful conversing.
Our communication was solid,
advanced even.
I expressed my needs and fears fully.
He made promises and I accepted.
He swore I was safe.
And I wanted to be safe.

I didn't know I was being fed lies.
What bystanders don't understand is
how his ability to lie to my face
and fake genuine love
was that of someone
who must not have a conscience.

Sociopath

I think you were telling me
the truth all along
when you said,
"I wonder if I might be a sociopath."
You weren't wondering.
You were temperature-checking
to make sure I'd still say,
"Of course you aren't.
A sociopath wouldn't have that worry!"

Mighty

I hate you.
I never thought I could.
But I was wrong.

My fire warms my bed where you used to.
I've become so strong.
But there was another way to bring me here.

Maybe nurture?
	stability?
	peace?

None of which you wanted to provide.
You like the infliction of pain.
Sadist.

Now I'm mighty.
But, god, I hate you.

Mystic

Even with all the tarot cards and crystal balls,
I would have never predicted how you'd go
from the love of my life to my life-destroyer.

I would have never employed my third eye
to see that you were abusing me.
Specs of manipulation seemingly isolated in the sky,
yet becoming intricate constellations over time
only an astronomer could discern.

I was so sure you were my fate.
That the three old ladies were resting easy,
since I had found you so early.

How stupid of me to think
I could do the fates' job for them.

Curriculum

When I did my courses,
I should have studied men like you.

All of this dissection in the lab
and no awareness that one day
I'd be laid out on the granite slab
as the human in human bio.

None the wiser that chemistry
is really just a bunch of gas.

They should have added you to the curriculum
so I knew how empires of love like mine fall.

So I could pinpoint the plagiarized words
of sweet nothings.

Understand the art behind
expertly sculpted facades.

Translate when someone speaks
the flowery language of manipulation.

You Are Not the Man I Loved

Calculate the difference
when things just don't add up.

My schooling prepared me
for many aspects of life.
But it certainly didn't prepare me
for you.

Therapy

I had therapy today,
and my therapist said,
"Jade, I am so sorry."

I cried about you today.
And even though I clawed at the pools
at the bottom of my eyes,
the tears spilled and burned as they ran down my cheeks,
scorching me anew and refreshing all the pain
you cared enough to bestow upon me
when you let yourself speak love
and leave me.

I don't always cry from my endeavors to be okay,
but it's probably 50/50.
...Okay, maybe it's more 75/25
with the score not in my favor.

Each week I go,
I'm more upset
that I'm still sitting in front of a laptop webcam
with you as the main topic.

You Are Not the Man I Loved

I don't know if you understand how much
I wish I could put you from my mind,
just as you put me from yours,
even while still holding my hand.

I feel finally released from your hex,
but I'm still choking from the smoke of it.

I'll schedule an appointment for next week.
I'll show up there, at my desk.
I'll speak of you again.
Maybe even cry.
And I'll hate each moment I'm still giving you.

Inventory

The time we spent was not the totality
of what you took from me.

You stole the seconds my heart spent
ripping in two...
then three...
then four.

You stole the minutes it took my brain
to compute my new reality.

The hours I spent questioning myself
and every chapter in our story.

You stole the days I spent locked in my apartment,
pounding fists on the floor.

The weeks of involuntarily living in flashbacks
at nearly every waking moment
and nightmares while asleep.

You Are Not the Man I Loved

You stole the months I spent trying to be okay.
Trying to rid myself of feeling things
that only caused me pain.

You've stolen a year,
and you're still stealing.

Though less frequent now,
you pop up to grab an hour
or a few moments as you can.
You reappear to show a prospect
why I can't believe anything they may say —
my tried-and-true ultimate trust issue.

You're the guilt-programed reason
receiving gifts induces anxiety.
Why I'm having to spend so much time
trying to learn that I'm worth something.
Trying to forgive myself
for loving someone so destructive.
Trying to convince myself
to listen to my intuition
because I'm so scared
I'll fall for someone like you again.

You color my poetry black.

You've changed me
into a different version of myself.

I'll never reacquaint myself with who I was
before I stepped into that pub,
sat down with you,
and ordered a fish and chips meal.
She deserved someone
who would receive her love
and pour back into her too.

The lessons you taught me
did not need to be taught.
I would have bloomed with love
that was love in practice
and not pain dressed up
in a top hat and tie.

BEGGING YOU

Sold

If I could remain frozen,
not go through days of defrost...

If I could move on
and skip the active healing process...

If I could wake up one day, in the future,
next to a man who really won't break my heart...

Hand me the contract
and flip to the last page.
I'll buy whatever you're selling.

Let Me Wager my Tears

Is there an amount of tears I could cry
to be done with this?
To be over the pain?
To move on and leave the hurt in the past,
a scar instead of a gaping wound
that refuses to heal?
Tell me the number of liters —
I can fill buckets.
Just make it stop hurting me.
Let me wager my tears.

Withdrawal

Tell me what the antidote is
for you.
Anything to release me from this withdrawal
of your love
that grips me in its claws
and squeezes.
Tell me what I can take to be free of a pain
so paralyzing,
so encompassing,
so poisonous,
that I'd rather suffer forever
if I could just pretend I'm fine.
If I could just keep taking my drug
and never have to be without you.

Sick

You've plagued me with the certainty
that I'll never be able to discern
the truth in what comes from your lips
or the intention behind your touch.
I must be sick
because I still want you to heal
and then knock again on my door,
so that I can eventually have
the very dream you destroyed.

Caged

It seems as if
instead of flying free,
all I want is to be caged
and fed with scraps of love
or scraps of something
I'm told is love.

Pause

All I want is a pause button —
an ethereal escape from my body.
And to come back months later,
when this is all over
and I don't have to grieve
every day of my existence.

You Are Not the Man I Loved

Love Heals All

A man who hates himself will hate you for loving him.

...So that's it — you despised me.

You were repulsed,
not by my pudge or my different interests
or my anxious little quirks,
but by the exclusive prize I awarded to you
straight from my chest.

You didn't love me because I loved you.
If you had, I wouldn't be broken now.
If you had loved me,
I would know what love feels like,
and guess what: I don't.
But if you had hated me,
I would know what love doesn't feel like.
And I can promise you I do.

I used to be romantic.
Hopeful.
— A hopeful romantic is the term.

You Are Not the Man I Loved

I'm not going to say I'm hopeless now,
but maybe math finally proved itself applicable in love
because statistically,
it's not that I'm hopeless,
it's that the odds just don't look good.
But when I was a hopeful romantic,
I bought that shit that love heals all.

It hadn't healed me,
and I didn't know at that point
me was the right place to start,
and my love was the love to heal myself with.
But I felt well-equipped to heal someone else.

All this love I had inside me was straining to come out,
and what happens sometimes
when you feel that yearning is that
instead of picking the right one, you pick the first.
The first one to show interest,
the first to kiss you,
the first to claim you,
and then the first rebound after the first one to claim you
returned you to the store.
And then the first ones who would accept a return.

You Are Not the Man I Loved

Almost New Condition.
Used: Very Good.
Used: Good.
Used: Acceptable.
Used: Poor.

I wasn't even in poor condition when you took me home.
But what can be made better can be made worse.

Women more than men, I think, get fed this lie that
we're here to make a man happy.
And having a man will make us happy.
But we don't stick around long enough to hear
the potential side effects
as they're read out off the screen.
— Or maybe because love isn't regulated by the FDA,
they don't even speed through them
at the end of the commercial.
Why would they?
Less women would buy.

So maybe most of us don't actually know that love can't fix
depression,
joblessness,
or a relationship where only one person is willing to try.

You Are Not the Man I Loved

One thing I've learned
is that despite all the love I carry in my vessel,
it does nothing if it's not received.
I can't love hard enough to make someone love themselves.
I've tried.
I've been dedicated to the cause.
And I've never been successful at loving someone hard enough
to love me for more than what I offer them.

Now I'm potentially discovering that you can love
hard enough to be hated.
And it all checks out.

He hated himself.
I tried to love him for both of us.

I sent myself back to the store:
Used: Poor.

M

The letter necklace I ordered,
when you and I were going to run away
and heal ourselves,
came in today.
It took so long
that there's no need for it now.
You're out of my life.
So I can't wear your initial
on my neck.
But do I give it away
or keep it
just in case
we really can heal
and one day run away?

The Key I Can't Lose

Even when I lock the door behind me,
I can't throw away the key.
I try to hide it,
but can't when I know where I left it.
Most times I can leave it there,
but most is not all.
When I'm feeling extra weak,
be it weak with hurt
or weak with anger,
I crack the door open,
just to take a peek.
And anytime the door's cracked,
it's twice as hard to close again.

You Are Not the Man I Loved

Hysteria

I ended up on top of you,
unintended after kisses of hysteria,
both of us desperate to love each other fully
after what you'd done to me.
Passion attempting fruitlessly to erase betrayal's stain.
And as I straddled,
passion turned to tears,
and sobs choked out that I loved you.
So much.
Broken and torn
by my very joy of being in this position at all.

You dried my eyes and loved me,
and I thought this was a first healing.
But at some point, you got up and showered.
And unbeknownst to me,
went on your way to deliver that very same love
to the other woman yet again,
as if mine washed off in the shower's steam.

Betrayal will always taste sweeter
to those who refuse to heal.

MOURNING YOU

Jack-O-Lantern

I don't want to feel hollow.
I can't carve more out of myself
like a jack-o-lantern,
paste on a fake smile,
and glow from a light inside
that isn't really mine.

Sweet Demise

I thought I was the poet between us.
But you spun my worries away
with lines that could have been penned
by the desires of my own heart.
And your poetry lulled me softly,
even sweetly,
to my demise.

You Are Not the Man I Loved

Even Though

I miss you,
even though
you broke me
in ways
I never knew
anyone could.

High Score

You weren't the first man to break me,
but you've got the high score.

The One

You told me I was the one.
But I wasn't just the one you loved.
I was the one you hated.
I was the one you played.
I was the one you seemed
determined to destroy.

In Case of Emergency

I loved you so long
that you were my emergency contact.

You loved me so little,
your best friend didn't know my name.

Or that we had a cat.
Or shared a living space.
Or a life.

Now I have to track down
every *in case of emergency*
that I filled out with your name
as the most important person in my life.

Because you showed me
I was the least important in yours.

Just Mine

You shut me out.
You moved on.
But you didn't even let me know
that your heart wasn't with your body.

Here I was,
loving you the whole time
you were no longer just mine.

Walk Away

I can discern your walk from a distance,
and you can discern mine.
It's crazy to me how
someone who knows me down to my gait
was so willing
to do the kind of harm to me
that would leave no option
but to watch me walk away.

Imposter

God —
I miss the person I thought you were.
Or maybe even used to be.
I didn't realize I got left
at some intersection on our journey,
and that someone else
stepped into your body
while still holding my hand.

Sleepless

I spent so many nights
sleepless over the years,
crying because you went out
and didn't make it home.
Calls went unanswered,
and I didn't know if you were alive
or dead.

I know now that I spent those nights,
unaware,
crying over you cheating.

Telemarketers

I caught the kind of love
where I saved our pictures as my background
so that I would always smile
when I picked up my phone.

You caught the kind of greed
where you unsaved my number
so you could blame my calls on telemarketers
to your other girlfriends.
And blame theirs on telemarketers to me.

I had yours saved with a heart.

Plaza Midwood

Your other girlfriend turned
a whole neighborhood against you.
But I had no one on my side
to save me from you.

Maybe I shouldn't have
let myself be hidden away.
I had no opportunity to
collect an ally from your side.

And I'm jealous someone else did.

City Shadows

I am so tired of this city.
Of minding my own business
and yet seeing you on every street corner
and in every establishment we graced together.

I'm tired of hiding from the shadows you leave.
Watching doors to ensure you haven't snuck in unannounced.
Freezing in my tracks
when a store security guard favors your profile.
Or shaking for an hour
after passing your car outside the apartment
of the woman who answered your work phone one evening
when your personal sent me straight to voicemail twice.

I miss when this city felt like my home.
When it was full of hope and so many possibilities of us.
When I didn't feel a victim of the colored skyline
that has always inspired awe from me.

I wish I didn't feel gnawing desperation
to abandon everything I've created over the years:
My home
My job
Daily routine
Friends

You Are Not the Man I Loved

But I do.

And I know there are those who tell me
I am strong enough to face the triggers.
I am.
I do.
But should I need to continue
if I'm afforded the opportunity to just go?

And no, I won't be running away from you,
even if it seems that you're the very reason I'm packing a bag.

The truth is:
I can't escape you.
I can't escape our past
or the stain you've left imprinted on:
My trust
My hope
My fears
My being

I haven't been able to leave the pain you've gifted me
at my doorstep,
my therapist's,
or yours.
And I know I won't be able to leave it in this city.

You Are Not the Man I Loved

But I think about walking around someone else
anywhere else
and not coming face-to-face with reminders
of the love I feel so stupid to have lent you.
I think about mining my potential
and living out the dreams I shared aloud
while curled up in your arms.

I won't ever seek you out to let you know I'm thriving
and doing all the things I said I was scared of doing.
But I think that in itself will be my satisfaction.
You don't get to know how I'm doing anymore,
be it bad or be it good.

All the shadows of mine you may meet here
— if you even think of me to see them —
will only be whispers of a version gone past.
A version of me you got to hold.
Who you no longer hold —
you'll never know her.

Traces

I can scrub my apartment,
replace my sheets,
donate everything with sentiment —
but you've marked this city with your scent,
and I won't be rid of you
until I'm able to crawl my way somewhere else.

The Stars Say

The stars say I'm a healer,
and I've never met someone so broken.
With all the love I could muster,
I only wished to kiss your wounds
and be there as they closed.

The stars say I'm a savior,
but I didn't want to save you.
Only to bear your problems with you
because I knew I wanted someone
who'd be willing to do the same.

The stars say I'm a protector,
but you can't face off with trauma.
So I focused on trying my hardest
to protect you from yourself.

But it turns out:
I was the one who needed protection.
I was the one who needed saving.
I am the one who now needs to heal.

Blue Hearts

Blue hearts remind me of you.
Your ex best friend
smothers me with them through text,
as she does her best to love me,
a stranger,
and help pick me back up
onto my feet,
after her best friend destroyed me
and betrayed her.

We mourn who we thought you were together.

Bleeding

You sought out emotional connections
while I sat here,
desperate to love you
with everything I ever had.

Maybe it if was just the sex,
I'd be better able to recover.
But I can't figure out how
there was ever room in our relationship
to need more than the love
I was bleeding for you.

I bled out.

Somatic

You don't understand how much my body hates you,
though my brain tells me I'm okay.
All that would happen if I saw you
is that I'd smirk and flip you off.
But my nervous system is still set off
when I see your car make and model
and the silhouette of someone who could be you.
The shakes still come.
My heart still threatens to eject itself.
"I'm okay."
"I'm okay,"
I have to tell myself.
You can't hurt me anymore.
I'm not that girl you played any longer —
even if you thought you saw her.

Allergies

My response to a sneeze,
when romantically involved,
is always a cheeky little: "Oh, are you allergic to me?"
They always say: "No, of course not!"

You can't be allergic to someone, of course.
Except I think that maybe you can.

You see, I think I'm allergic to you.
It's not the sneezes,
but it's the shakes.
It's my heart pounding in its cage
as if it's trying to win a chariot race,
picking up the pace,
faster and faster and faster and faster,
and I know I'm out of harm's way,
but when I see you —
or someone you favor —
even your silver car make and model,
the driver unknown inside:
My body reacts.

I can't control it the same way you can't control a sneeze.
Or if so, barely,
where suppression still takes over your senses
with a creeping pressure across your sinuses
that doesn't know how to disperse
and a prickling saltwater arrival at the corner of your eyes.

I'm allergic.
No longer to your bullshit —
I got prescribed the cure for that:
It was truth and a hefty spoonful of self-respect,
forced down my throat by nothing more
than the all-encompassing pain
of being destroyed from the inside.

I'm allergic to you.
Your presence.
Your possibility of presence.
Hell, I'm allergic to you as a concept.
I'm allergic to the way you made me feel all those years
you abused me and called it love.
I'm allergic to the reminder of all the ways you abused me
and the way I accepted it as love:
Every single time.

You Are Not the Man I Loved

I'm allergic to knowing that you're treating others
the same way you treated me.
That one makes me sneeze.

I've sneezed a few times.
A sneezing fit back when the cure started working,
my body getting hit at once
with truth-side effects in rapid succession
while uncovering like clockwork every other day
a new woman,
unconsciously bound to me in trauma and in sexual health.
Achoo!
Achoo!
Achoo!
Achoo!
Achoo!

And then occasional sneezes here and there.
A sneeze called: "I thought he was single."
Achoo!
A sneeze called: "He keeps trying to take me out."
Achoo!
A sneeze called: "I promise I didn't know,
but this explains a lot."

Achoo!
A sneeze called: "He said that I was his person too."
Achoo!
And a sneeze almost two years later, out of the blue,
after I thought the side effects had finally worn off:
"Hi, you don't know me,
and I don't mean to stall your healing in any way,
but I wanted to let you know he's still the exact same."

Other women,
other relationships,
one more receiver of high-risk HPV.
Achoo!
Achoo!
A-fucking-choo.

You can clear HPV when you catch it early,
but you can't really cure allergies, can you?
You just avoid the irritants.
And I try my best to,
but unfortunately,
I think I'll always be allergic to everything to do with you.

Operating Table

It makes sense now
why,
when I signed up to be
childless
on an operating table,
he made sure it wasn't for him,
but for me.

Because while they cut me open,
under bright lights
to go inside,
he skipped out on the waiting room,
opened and went inside
the body of
another woman.

Dissociation

Dissociation was the final thing you gifted me,
as the trauma you had been so generous
to send my way
overwhelmed my nervous system
to the point of desperate escape.

I cannot count it as my favorite gift,
though the numbness of feeling
disconnected from my core
more or less saved me on occasion
from another soul-shattering breakdown
as my mind conveniently opted out.

I gave you a love like no other.
You: The ethereal experience
of floating outside myself.

I suppose you could say
I changed by loving you.

Siren

Lies of love was the song you sang
and then encored thrice.
The melody was so hypnotizing
coming from your lips.
How could I know that pain
sounded so beautiful?
In my life, you were the siren,
and I played the sailor.
I kept pulling my head up
out of the waves,
only to let you drown me
again
and again.
Now I'm free from the music,
but I find the ocean's silence
to be crippling.

Pleasure

The need to feel pleasure right now,
in some form,
is overwhelming.
Maybe it's because
all that's on my mind is that
I'll never again receive my pleasure
from you.

Five years of learning
how to love each other's bodies,
and now I'll have to start over
with someone else one day.
A new lesson
and a new lesson plan.

Dreams

Even my dreams know I love you still.
When I close my eyes to sleep,
I can no longer remind myself
that you're this monster
that utterly devoured me in reality.

It was nice to see you again.
To be loved by you again.
Even if only in my dreams.

And maybe I even hope
that I might see you there again.

Thief

You stole my soul with a kiss,
and I thought I was falling in love.

Trauma Bond

I am so sorry.
I loved him too.
I know he broke us.
How painful it is that it was all a lie.
But as much as I have tried,
my soul just can't bear to hear
one more time
how you thought my person
was your person too.

Poisoned Hands

I hate that when my heart was breaking
into a hundred pieces,
only to break into a thousand more,
I didn't give myself the credit that I'd live through it.
I thought this man and his poisoned hands would break me.
That I would suffocate without the love of a man
who never truly loved me.

I came into my inner child,
and I let her take hold,
knowing I was wronging her.
She deserved and needed my protection,
and I didn't give it.
I didn't step up because I felt like I was being swallowed
by a tsunami of pain
that left me stripped of everything I knew
and stole the person that I loved.

I didn't show up.

Maybe she'll forgive me.
I had promised I'd protect her —
that I'd keep her safe.
And maybe now,
now that I'm full and no longer walking around
with a gaping hole from a man with poisoned hands,
reaching out and taking my love to fill his own,
maybe now I can apologize to Little Me.
I can tell her it won't always be okay in the moment,
but we will always come through.
Even if I'm late, I'll still protect you.
Through the worst, we're whole.

Dust

I've been your breaking point
for everything done to you by others before.
I came around —
right intentions,
but still flawed.
I tripped the sensors set
to a hyper-sensitivity
no one could have avoided.
Now I'm all burned up
by the laser system you armed
for a thief in a museum,
when I was just there to dust.

Rot

I don't think I'm being dramatic when I say:
I want to rot.
Because while I don't wish myself harm,
I'd very much like to
cross my legs,
place my hands on my knees,
clear my mind,
and sit here until my body breaks down
and returns from whence it came.

Human

It was easier when I thought you were hateable.
You are despicable.
But you are also a human.
A human I loved more than any other.
At the core of my being,
I don't even think I'm capable
of hating someone who once had my heart.
But it would spare mine if I was.

Freedom

You claimed you worried
that you were an anchor on my ship.
I did everything to not let you believe it.
But I was treading water trying to bring you with me.
Now that you're gone,
all I have to do is set sail.
But instead,
I'm just drifting.
Freedom doesn't taste the same
without the one I thought would share it with me.

Demo

I'm getting berated with comments from people
trying to tell me it was all bad.
Questioning why I even stuck around.
Throwing jabs about my treatment.

But I had everything once.

Isn't that how it always happens?
A man sells you your dream with a demo,
and you've never known life could be so good.
Then he takes it away,
piece by piece,
until you're begging for the minimum.
Hooked on the demonstration of the past
that proves it could be yours again
if you just hang on.

Lemonade

I do not want any more hard lessons.
Not one more soul-breaking,
body-dehydrating lesson.
No more silver linings.
No more lemonade.
I just want love.
...And maybe the lesson that I can have it.

The Girl I Thought You Loved

How can you say you love me
and do the one thing I told you
would hurt me most?

How easy was it
to kill the girl
I thought you loved?

One Last Meal

One last meal before you're gone forever.
They say on death row, you get to pick.
You picked for me:
Grilled cheese and tomato soup.
Because it's comforting.
In prison, they probably don't get to watch
as the meal is prepared.
I did.
And it tasted sadder than the dish.

It tasted like the memories of a hundred meals
we cooked together over the years:
The pasta dough you'd make from scratch.
A slow-cooked Bolognese: Four hours minimum.
Kabobs on an old grill grate rehomed to the fire pit.
It tasted like the deviled eggs I over-salted one Easter
when we just stayed home and watched a movie.
It tasted like the chicken you fried
that convinced me to abandon pescetarianism.
Like the fried Oreos we made on our third date,
the day I thought to myself
that you were my future figured out.

One last meal before you're gone forever.
One last scene of it being prepared.

Remnants

I still find you —
pieces of you.
Remnants of our life together.

It was once natural integration;
now it's like an infection I can't rid from my body.

The photos,
videos,
mementos,
the theme park ticket stubs
...and apparently old voicemails from blocked numbers.

Your voice hurts to hear.

I used to love it so deeply.
When I listen now,
the familiarity of your inflections,
pauses,
and the way you say my name,
reaches into my chest and grips
with the tightness of a muscle
that hasn't been stretched in months.

You used to use that voice to love me.

You used to tell me in that voice everything I wanted to hear.
And you sold it with the tact of a veteran salesman,
bringing home a large commission.

Do me a favor and forget my number.

Though you can't, can you?
Because you committed it to memory
so that it could float around without a name attached.

"It's just a telemarketer calling."
"They won't leave me alone."

Now I need you to leave me alone.
Leave me alone so that in time I can forget your voice.
Forget the familiarity of your inflections.
Your pauses.
The way you say my name.

And how it sounded to hear you say you loved me.

MOVING ON FROM YOU

Have I Arrived?

I may be tasting peace
for the first time in so long.
Have I processed this trauma enough
to have finally landed in Acceptance?
Or will I wake up tomorrow,
just as broken as before?

The Me Who Loved You

I don't fear running into you —
I fear facing off with the me who loved you.
The scared, abused version of myself
who shrunk 10 times smaller than should be possible
to keep someone around who only destroyed her.

I outgrew her.
But I'm scared she might still live in me.
If she were to come out...
could I protect her now?

If Only

I've spent time with *If Only*.
But now I'm assured
that there's nothing I could have done
to love you harder
than I already did.
There was nothing in me
unreceptive to your heart.
I can't change a narrative you dictated
without being told the story
playing in your head.
I could never be perfect enough
to not be imperfect.
This wasn't in me;
it was in you.

Access

My problem is:
I didn't cage my heart
and make you earn the key.
I allowed full access,
just hoping you'd love me
because you said you wouldn't hurt me.

The next will earn the key.

Disposable

There was nothing I could have done
to prove I was worth loving
when you had already determined
that I was disposable.

Unequivocal

The love you had from me
was unequivocal.
The love you gave back:
Manufactured.
I won't lie and say I'm not suffering.
But you'll suffer more the day
it finally dawns on you
that I was everything
that could have made you truly happy.

You Don't Deserve Me

The next man who tells me
he doesn't deserve me
and I'd be better off without him,
I'll believe.

I spent years trying to convince you
you were wrong.
That you were lovable.
Worthy.
Deserving of me.

But you knew the whole time
that you weren't,
and you told me.
I was trying to convince myself.

Detox

I was convinced
that if we weren't fated to be together,
being apart from you would kill me.

I would have never imagined
that parting from you
would actually save me.

You weren't who I thought you were.
You were a poison.
This is detox.

Collection of Women

When you picked the type of women you wanted to love you,
you might as well have selected *copy* and *paste*.
Not only in looks, but in how loving we are.
How nurturing and kind.
Understanding to a fault.
Queens of support and authentic connection.

But now we're supporting ourselves
– and each other.
You collected women who get each other.
Lovers of therapy and validation.
You gifted us the removal of your manipulation
– and gifted us each other.

Confidence

You picked apart every piece of me,
slowly over time.
But I don't know if you expected that
each piece you removed,
I'd put back.

And after meeting multiple women
you put into the game,
without ever subbing me out,
I think they're beautiful,
but I know I'm beautiful too.

ROI

I am going to collect lessons from you
until the lessons run out.
Anything to pocket that I can charge
against the cost of our relationship
to end up with a less staggering loss.
You fumbled the opportunity of me.
And I'm a bad investor.

Statistically

I see his car, but I tell myself:
It isn't his.
Statistically it isn't him.
Sometimes the vehicle that speeds up my pulse
isn't even the same make or model –
just a brand that starts with *H*.

It works.
Statistically, every time, it was never his.
At least every time for the last year.

I saw another tonight.
"It isn't his," my trained brain said.
But the vehicle tonight had a dent in the side,
on the left, near the wheel.
And the right *H* logo.

And it wasn't his, as probability would dictate.
But here I am, pulse racing,
thankful it isn't him,
but sitting in the math
that still one silver, rear-dented sedan in this city is.

Where I Water

Someday I'll stop spilling tears
over the pain you've caused me,
and instead I'll water a man who heals me
with the safe space he provides emotionally.

The Difference

You hurt because you could.
I loved because I could.

Do you see the difference between us?

Art

What I'm thankful for,
amidst it all,
is to be a creative.
I can't take back
the five years I gave you
or regret them fully
because I love who I turned into.
But from the pain you lent me,
I can at least make art.

His Other Lover

How do we describe our relationship when we go out
and have a drink with strangers?
Friends.

But how did we meet?
We were brought together.

How so?
Interesting circumstances.

What kind of circumstances?
*We loved the same man
and he broke us.*

But now we have each other instead.
Isn't that beautiful?

3/24/2024

He Loves Me

He loves me not.

Did you love me
or did you not?

You want me to think you did.
You still call from unblocked numbers
to say it should have been me.

But it wasn't.

I loved you.
You loved me not.

I won't give in to your convincing
to be the absolution of your guilt.

Vampiric

I thought it was safe
to let you exhaust my resources.
While I knew it wasn't smart,
I thought you wouldn't do me dirty.
A sacrifice of love for the one I loved most.
An investment in our future.
Proof of the very dedication I held
for the love of my life.

You weren't safe —
You were a thief wearing a janitor's jumpsuit.
I thought you were here to clean out my traumas.
But instead, you cleaned me out
of everything I was eager to offer.

Today I thought of Venmo requesting
a little of what I gave up.
But the money is nothing in comparison
to the love you sucked from my arteries
when I gave you access to everything
...including my heart.

Unmasked

I broke free.
You're unmasked.
I recognize you now
as the stranger you've always been.
If you'd never donned the mask,
I never would have shared my love.
I won't call you a monster,
though you may be a fiend.
Now you're just someone I don't know
and could never understand.

You don't want peace,
but I do.
So savor the chaos you've reaped
because for me, your chapter has closed.

Unsolicited Ads

I'm tired of you haunting me,
inserting unsolicited reflection
into moments of content
that six months ago,
I never knew I'd see so soon.

Memories of you and your aggravations
flash like ads,
interrupting the scheduled programing
of me enjoying the life
I'm cultivating without you.

Do I need to be still reminded
of the multitude of ways you harmed me
when I have already submitted
my acknowledgement of receipt?

Is there yet more to process?
Or are these glimpses serving to remind me
how far I've come
and what to ensure I no longer accept?

I won't so easily forget this pain.
You are my lesson.

Hunted

Somehow,
within the coolness of your blood
exists a power to sense
when I am most at peace in this world.
A sensor for you to orchestrate
the smallest reemergence.
To punish me with a stabbing reminder
that I once let you in enough
to wound my core.
You taunt that I cannot escape you,
even if continents away.
I am hunted.

For how long?

Quivers

Yesterday I learned how it felt to be carved
when local anesthesia wasn't given enough time
before blade met flesh.
And even though I was drugged,
I was awake
and shook in my self-imposed restraints.

It was like being under your manipulation tactics
and how I chained myself
to a man who wanted to harm me
just to see the quivers of his power.

For my surgeon, once he started,
he couldn't let me bleed out.
For you, my blood only motivated —
assured you that I would survive your harm
and give you what you wanted.

I laid on the table,
the sounds and pulls of my skin diluting the valium.
And though I shook and whimpered,
I knew this pain was for my betterment.
The cuts you made were only for yours.

You Are Not the Man I Loved

I didn't cry.
I was comforted by a nurse's hand on my head
and the satisfaction that the scars I earned from you —
when my initial healing was derailed by the grief
of finding my love bare in a space with another —
this pain was erasing those physical reminders.
They were being carved out.

You won't get a chance to hurt me anymore.

Early Parole

There is one night specifically
that I keep coming back to,
even the majority of a year later.
My brain gets snagged in this memory,
distraught at being so close
yet not uncovering the truth,
and fantasizing about changing it.

I should have asked the right questions
instead of hoping a regular
would volunteer what I needed to know
from vague questioning of the two of you,
sitting together on the floor under the bar,
as I remained out of view.

I think of how many months of freedom
early parole would have granted
if I had seen your lies that night
instead of absorbing your justifications
because I wanted the truth to be
that you loved me.

You Are Not the Man I Loved

How much more healed could I be
at this moment in time right now
if I had been more willing to see your malice
and less willing to power my intuition down?

I was so close that night
to meeting who I was actually dating
and discovering:
You are not the man I loved.

Unlike You

I met another man unlike you —
one to heal a tiny piece of me
looking for you in every man
and terrified of finding you.

You Are Not the Man I Loved

Belgium

I want to say I don't know when
my life switched to what it is today,
bussing back from Belgium
when I only meant to stay a day.
Yet I adopted a new toothbrush
and crawled into a strange man's bed.

But I do know when.
It started when you broke me,
and between never-ending tears
and a constant mild high CBD could provide,
I yearned for the next version of me.
I broke down because I wasn't her fast enough.

And here I am.
A goddess you tamed and caged
before I even tasted what my own power could be.

I smile at blurred countryside going by
because I should be at work
at 3:30 pm on the East Coast.

You Are Not the Man I Loved

But it's 9:30 at night,
and I fucked the most gorgeous man last night.
And again this morning.
My thong is soaked in my bag.

I might come to Belgium again.
I feel powerful.
Grateful for this life.
Happy you're gone.
Relieved I'm free.
Basking in uncovering my sexuality.
Discovering the goddess I am —
with my cage door wide open.

Biggest Mistake

If I received the question,
"What has been your biggest mistake?"
the first thing that comes to mind is you.
How could you not?
You're the definition of the word.
My trauma whispers as much when I can't sleep.
When I can sleep even, visiting my dreams.
It's the soundtrack of my flashbacks.
It whispers *mistake* in stilled silence
and when a man wants to love me but I'm too afraid.
But can you be a mistake
when I needed to learn a lesson?
When nothing else but a wounded heart set on fire
could have been my teacher?
In so many ways you were my biggest mistake.
Yet you taught me to stop abandoning myself.

You Are Not the Man I Loved

S-Anon

I went to S-Anon after I found him cheating.
He tried to steal my anger by saying he had a problem.
Was it an affliction I could handle?
He showed me his newly bought workbook,
and I decided I'd try to.

Though nothing in me understood,
I bought my own book,
searching for the reason why his lust for flesh
was stronger than his love for me.

We consulted with a therapist
for a three-thousand-dollar weekend intensive.
I wanted to see if we were savable.
He told her there was just the prostitute I had met.

But it wasn't just the sex worker.
She stole his wallet on the way out,
after I assured her she didn't have my anger.
An act of solidarity for me, I tend to think.

And it wasn't just the girlfriend of half a year.
She left him at an Alabama gas station
when she picked up my call to his phone,
while he drove her back from a trip
that was supposed to be with me.

You Are Not the Man I Loved

It wasn't just the college friend he told me not to worry about.
"You'd love her," he said.
But he left out: "I fucked her."
He was right though — I do love her.

And it wasn't just any of the ten plus others.

I stayed in S-Anon awhile, trying to heal.
I went to group weekly.
There were 12 steps.
We read a kind of culty intro every time.

We never said names of the people who'd sent us there.
We took responsibility as codependents,
somehow acting as an accomplice
to an ethics violation we hadn't known the existence of.
Sex addiction was a sickness.

This is how they tried to steal my anger.

I asked one week:
"Why can't I feel anger? I only feel grief."
They said: "Anger is loss cooked up with hot sauce."

All I wanted was to stop feeling loss and to just feel angry.
Yet I spent so much time trying to turn hurt into a lesson
so I could make my anger productive.
To make anger work for me,
so as to not be employed by it.

But when I tell friends this part of my lore,
they call it a movie plot.
Some fantasize about running into him.
Some dream of dealing a face punch — just for me.
I used to be terrified of a run in.

I wasn't a codependent enabler.
I wasn't somehow encouraging him to betray me every week.
I wasn't responsible for dealing my own pain.
He just made an excuse to try to steal my anger.

Now if he runs into me,
he'll get to glimpse a new version.
He'll get to glimpse my confidence.
My happiness.
Two new tattoos.

I found my anger.
Now I've found my peace.

Ghosts

I had to leave home.
The ghosts were just too loud.
It turns out they know the city better than I do.
They hid on every street corner
and look like men who favor you.
They were so loud
and everywhere.
I had to leave home;
spend time away.
But I've come back,
and my ghosts have quieted now.
It seems like home could be home again.

Only For Me

I remember you saying you were proud of me
for taking steps to actualize my dreams.

I'm climbing the stairs,
but you're not here to see it.
It doesn't matter anymore if you're proud.

But I want you to know
that my dreams didn't stall
because of how you hurt me.

Your cruelty didn't crush my will
to make something of my life
beyond what I've been living.

I could have been sharing this adventure
with you.
But I'm doing it on my own.

And it'll be a fuller experience now
that I'm only doing it for me,
and doing none of it for you.

The Other Side of Survival

Every time I close my eyes, I find myself smiling.
How did life get so good that content bombards me
as soon as I've loosened visual distractions?
There's no escaping how good it feels to be alive.
How incredible it feels on the other side of survival.

The nights on the floor with fistfuls of carpet,
the moments I was ripping apart internally,
waiting with urgency to meet myself today —
they're finally just memories.
The starkest contrast I could have ever imagined.

I used to dissociate and pray I was in a coma.
That I'd wake up and reality would melt away.
Now I'm living a dream without a need to awaken.

Sunflower

I once asked my ex what color I was,
and he said yellow.
He said I was spring and a sunny day.
If I was a flower, I'd be a sunflower.

At the time, I assumed he loved me.
We'd been together for so long,
and he said he loved me.

But he didn't.
I know that now, and I'm okay,
even though for weeks and months I wasn't.
For a tumultuous time I thought I wasn't good enough,
perfect enough,
lovable enough.

But I was.
And I am.
He just wasn't capable of loving me.
I accept it now.
I'm learning to bloom through the pain.

But even though all he was to me was lies
and a curated lover,
I am still yellow.
I am still spring.
I am still a sunny day.
I am still a sunflower.

Even he could see that.

You Don't Have to Handle This Alone

If this book has triggered memories, emotions, or experiences that feel overwhelming, please know that support exists.

Betrayal, emotional abuse, and prolonged grief can deeply affect the nervous system, sense of self, and ability to trust. These responses are not personal shortcomings — they are human. You deserve care while navigating them.

Here are some places you can turn to:

For US Readers

- **988 Suicide & Crisis Lifeline:**
  Call or text 988

- **Crisis Textline:**
  Text HOME to 741741

- **National Domestic Violence Hotline**
  1-800-799-SAFE (7233) or thehotline.org
  (Support includes emotional abuse and coercive relationships, even without physical violence.)

For International Readers

- A global directory of crisis and suicide prevention resources can be found by country at: findahelpline. com

If you are able, working with a licensed therapist, especially one trained in trauma or abuse recovery, can be profoundly supportive. You don't have to handle this alone.

Meet the Poet

Jade Divac is a confessional free verse poet. She writes wherever she wanders, capturing the quiet truths we often carry but may not speak aloud.

Her work is shaped by heartbreak, healing, and the raw honesty of being fully human. She invites readers to feel without apology. To sit with sorrow, longing, and love, and to hold each emotion with gentleness before letting go.

She finds comfort in the hum of airports and the chaos of movement, often scribbling poems on planes and in places she's never been before. She often holds a passport in one hand and her heart cracked open in the other.

She uses poetry to process and honor emotions, especially the messy ones. She believes that when we gather the strength to speak from our softest places, we give others encouragement to do the same.

Follow the Writer

For more poetry, book updates,
and glimpses behind the pages
– follow @jadedivac
www.jadedivac.com

Also by Jade Divac

Emote

More to Come

Bedsheets & Moonbeams

Erotica with a pulse. Poetry with a bite.
Pleasure written like scripture
for those who long to be
wrecked and revered.

Acknowledgements

To my artist and stolen friend, Janelle Bouchard – You took on a project that was not only my pain, but also yours. Thank you for taking a part not only in the project, but for mentoring me through the most painful heartbreak of my life. Your shared experience, unlimited compassion for me, and immediate and continuous love for me forged the version of me able to get through. Our friendship was created out of pain but refused the limitations of that container.

To my editor, Vanessa Dremé — Your critique, feedback, and enthusiasm are vital resources for me. You have held heavy piece after heavy piece with care and honesty, and that itself is no small task.

To my designers and early readers — Thank you for your time, your eyes, your honesty, and your care. Your hand in this work helped carry it to its final form.

To my village, those who witnessed the shattering and those who came after — You taught me everything about love when I no longer knew if the word had meaning. You let me break and let me heal without ever telling me I was too much. You held sadness on my behalf, anger on my behalf, and you held *me*. The only reason I believe in love still is because of you.

And to the man I loved but didn't actually know — You have no claim to the person I am or the art I make because of you, directly or indirectly. If Hell is real, it was made for you.

I could apologize for the heaviness of this book, but instead I'm going to thank you. Thank you for holding it. Thank you for sitting with something I created in order to survive. I am not unaware that while the trauma that shaped these pieces was heavy for me to process, it is also heavy to witness. Experiencing this book is an act of love in itself. Thank you for gifting that.

Writing this book hurt, even in its final stages, two years later. I am no longer the version of myself who loved this man, but the damage done to my nervous system and belief system was comprehensive. But if placing *You Are Not The Man I Loved* into someone's hands helps them feel less alone with their pain, if it offers even a quiet *I understand*, that is all I wish to alchemize from this.

You are not alone in feeling swallowed by emotion. You are not behind because you find yourself slipping back into stages of grief you think you should have outgrown. It hurts because it must, and it must because feeling is a part of getting through. There is no timeline. There are no levels to graduate from. You are not weak for feeling the impact of betrayal. And if you can't wrap your head around how someone could do this to you — good. You are not required to learn how to sympathize with a devil.